DON'T POP YOUR CORK ON MONDAYS!

WRITTEN BY ADOLPH MOSER, Ed.D.

ILLUSTRATED BY DAV PILKEY

THE CHILDREN'S ANTI-STRESS BOOK

LANDMARK EDITIONS, INC.

P.O. Box 4469   1402 Kansas Avenue   Kansas City, Missouri 64127

Sixth Printing

TEXT: COPYRIGHT© 1988 BY ADOLPH J. MOSER, Ed.D.

ILLUSTRATIONS: COPYRIGHT© 1988 BY DAV PILKEY

International Standard Book Number: 0-933849-18-4 (LIB. BDG.)

Library of Congress Cataloging-in-Publication Data
Moser, Adolph J., 1938-
  Don't pop your cork on Mondays!
  "The children's anti-stress book."
  Summary: Explores the causes and effects of stress and offers practical
approaches and techniques for dealing with stress in daily life.
  1. Stress (Psychology) — Juvenile literature.
  2. Stress management — Juvenile literature.
  [1. Stress (Psychology)   2. Stress management]
I. Pilkey, Dav, 1966-   ill.   II. Title.
BF575.S75M68   1988   155.9   88-13912

Editorial Coordinator: Nancy R. Thatch
Creative Coordinator: David Melton

Landmark Editions, Inc.
P.O. Box 4469
1402 Kansas Avenue
Kansas City, Missouri 64127
(816) 241-4919

Printed in the United States of America

Dedicated to
two occasional "cork poppers,"
Scott and Leta,
with googols of love.

PREFACE

Stress-related disorders now rank as our nation's single most prominent health problem. Because these disorders can strike anyone, regardless of his or her age, stress has indeed become a household word throughout the United States.

Adults are greatly concerned about stress in their lives. They worry about it, talk about it, write about it, listen to tapes about it, read about it, and lose sleep over it. Some adults attend workshops and seminars. Others seek professional help. Still others change jobs, or dissolve marriages, or argue with their neighbors, or yell at anyone who is within earshot.

Children too must contend with stress in today's rapidly changing, highly pressurized world. Only in recent years, however, have adults begun to fully realize the vast numbers of children involved and the enormous impact that stress is having on their lives. It is estimated that one half of all children in the United States now suffer from some type of stress-related disorder. What is even more startling is that younger and younger children are being affected by stress.

Although we adults take our own stress seriously, we are prone to assume that stress factors in the lives of children are minor when compared to ours. To us, passing a math test doesn't seem as important as climbing the corporate ladder. We tend to believe that peer pressure between children is not as disruptive as conflicts we have with co-workers. Too often we consider our children's problems to be no more than emotional mole hills. To the contrary, the stresses young people encounter within their range of experiences can present traumatic mountains for them to scale.

As a psychologist who has worked with stress-related problems in hundreds of children and their families, I can assure you, it is vital to the good health and well-being of children for them to understand stress and to develop stress survival skills. Once learned, these skills can help children to control, cope with, avoid and eliminate stress factors in their lives.

To teach stress survival skills to children, we begin by discussing types of stress factors and their causes. Then we proceed to explore how stress affects our mental and physical attitudes. After that we can address effective methods for dealing with stressful situations.

It is important for children to understand that they are not alone in feeling the pressures of our fast-paced society — that everyone can suffer from stress. Most importantly, children should be made aware that people are not helpless in combating stress — that there are ways to recognize stress factors, and there are methods by which we can reduce, and even overcome, many pressures. And that is precisely what this book is about.

How you present DON'T POP YOUR CORK ON MONDAYS! to your children is your choice. However, to get the most from the book, I suggest that you and your children take the time to read it together. As you turn the pages, you will begin to understand the pressures that affect your children, and your children will have the opportunity to consider your problems.

Also participate with your children in doing the stress-reducing exercises in the book. All of you will benefit from these relaxing techniques, because the exercises are not only effective — they are also fun to do.

Mutual growth of understanding and concern can help you to strengthen the support system in your family. Through caring and sharing, you and your children can reduce stress and work together to improve the quality of life for every member of your family.

Read. Enjoy. Grow.

Adolph Moser

It happens every day—
some people come unstrung.
They pop their corks,
they start to yell,
and they begin to
act like animals.

Some people who are under stress
growl and snarl like lions.

Others act like monkeys
and "go bananas!"

Still others lose control
and act like bulls.
They smash everything in sight.

Some people who are under stress
don't yell and scream at all.
They simply refuse to face a problem,
and, like ostriches,
bury their heads in the sand.
Sometimes people cry,
or they want to run away.

Others become very quiet,
and, just like turtles,
crawl into their shells.

At one time or another,
stress affects everyone—
It affects grocers and bakers,
and football players,
cab drivers, teachers,
and street workers too.

Mothers are affected by stress,
and so are fathers.

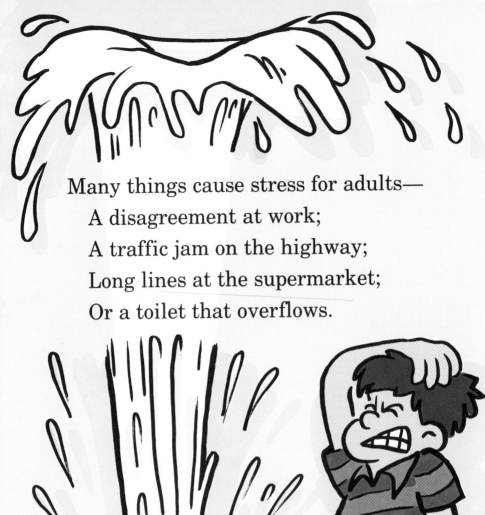

Many things cause stress for adults—
A disagreement at work;
A traffic jam on the highway;
Long lines at the supermarket;
Or a toilet that overflows.

Or, sometimes adults have
more work to do than they can handle.

Or they lose their jobs.
Or there isn't enough money
to pay the bills
and buy the things they need.

One of the worst things about stress
is that it's often passed on
from one person to another.
If business is poor,
the boss gets upset
and yells at an employee.
During lunch, the employee
is rude to a waitress.

The waitress goes home that night
and scolds her children.

Finally, the children yell at the dog.
But what's a poor dog to do?

When adults are under stress,
some of them lose control.
They may say awful things.
They can even become dangerous,
and sometimes, they hit people.
When adults act this way,
it is very wise to back off
and give them time and space
to blow off steam.

Children are affected by stress too.
You feel stressed out when:
    You can't understand your
    homework assignment;
    Or you've forgotten to study for a big test;
    Or your best friend won't speak to you;
    Or other kids pick on you,
    or they completely ignore you.
    Or when...
        you're too tall, too short,
        too fat, too thin,
        too young, or too old.

You also get stressed out
when your parents scream and argue,
or when your parents don't take time
to listen to your problems.

So stress affects us all,
and it has since time began.
Long, long ago,
our cavemen relatives
experienced stress.
While they hunted for food,
a hungry bear or tiger
might suddenly attack them.

This caused tremendous stress!
Suddenly, hundreds of changes
occurred inside their bodies—
Their hearts pounded faster,
and energy rushed to their muscles.
Instantly, they were ready to fight
or to run for safety.

Today, people are rarely
attacked by tigers or bears.

Instead, we worry about—

"Will I arrive at school on time?"

Or..."Will I make a passing grade?"

And..."What will happen to me if I don't?"

These fears are not life or death threats—
they are psychological threats.
But our nervous systems don't always
know the difference,
so we react to these threats
in much the same way
our ancestors reacted
when wild animals attacked them.

Some stress can be good for us.
It can help us to become more alert
and to be more careful.
When we cross a busy street,
stress can make us more cautious.

When we are anxious about passing a test,
stress urges us to study more.
If we're determined to win a sports contest,
stress makes us practice harder.

When we are under stress,
our muscles get a big dose
of extra energy
that prepares us to fight or run.
But how can we physically
fight a pop quiz? We can't.
And we can't run away from it either.

Because we don't burn up the
extra energy in our muscles,
our bodies become tense,
our hearts pound faster,
and we worry and fret.
We may start feeling very tired.
We can even become sick.

However, the very next time
you feel uptight —
like your spring is sprung,
or you're just not right;
when you're mad as a hornet,
or sweating from fright;

or you can't get to sleep,
and it's late at night;
when you're red-faced with anger,
and your cork's going to pop—

STOP!

There ARE ways you can reduce stress
if you learn how.

Before things get out of hand,
EXERCISE YOUR TENSION AWAY!
Burn off that extra energy —
RUN! SWIM! JUMP ROPE!
PEDAL A BIKE!

DO SIT-UPS! RIDE A SKATEBOARD!
TAKE A WHACK AT A BASEBALL!
DANCE! SING! TWIST AND SHOUT!
RELEASE THE STRESS!
LET IT ALL OUT!

Or...SHAKE YOUR TENSION AWAY!
Pretend you're a playful wet puppy.
WIGGLE and JIGGLE,
and SHAKE ALL OVER!
As imaginary drops of water
fly in every direction,
you'll feel the tension leave your body.

Another fun way to release stress
is to OUT-TENSION THE TENSION!
Next time your muscles feel tight,
TIGHTEN them even more!
Start with your feet.
Curl your toes into a TIGHT ball.
Feel the tension build.

Now TIGHTEN your legs,
then your stomach,
then your chest.
Now TIGHTEN your hands,
your arms, your shoulders,
your neck...your face...your head.
From the tips of your toes,
to the tops of your eyebrows—
your muscles are TIGHT WITH TENSION!
HOLD IT!
COUNT TO FIVE — 1 - 2 - 3 - 4 - 5.

Now RELEASE every part of your body.
Let all the tension go...
RELAX...RELAX...RELAX
until you're as limp as a rag doll.

Or...BREATHE YOUR STRESS AWAY.

Lie down in a quiet place.

Close your eyes,

and place your hands over your ribs.

Think of your belly as a balloon.

TAKE A DEEP BREATH.

BREATHE IN SLOWLY through your nose

until the balloon feels full.

HOLD IT.

COUNT TO FIVE — 1 - 2 - 3 - 4 - 5.

> Then BREATHE OUT SLOWLY
>
> through your mouth.
>
> Repeat the exercise several times.
>
> Each time you will become
>
> more and more RELAXED.

Now...
Pretend you're a butterfly
floating on the breeze.
Imagine a peaceful meadow
where beautiful flowers gently sway.
Feel warm sunlight flow through your veins.

Tell yourself—
  "My whole body is warm and comfortable.
  I am calm and relaxed.
  Because I am calm and relaxed,
  everything is okay.
  I can handle any problem."

Relaxing may not solve every problem,
but once you relax,
problems won't seem quite so big,
and it will be easier to solve them.

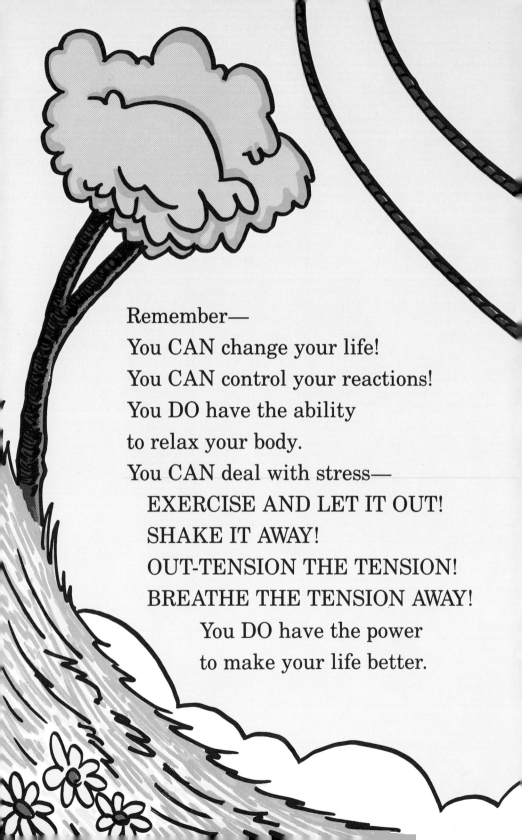

Remember—
You CAN change your life!
You CAN control your reactions!
You DO have the ability
to relax your body.
You CAN deal with stress—
EXERCISE AND LET IT OUT!
SHAKE IT AWAY!
OUT-TENSION THE TENSION!
BREATHE THE TENSION AWAY!
You DO have the power
to make your life better.

So—
Don't pop your cork on Mondays!
On Tuesdays, keep your cool.
Always stay calm on Wednesdays.
Thursdays...don't play the fool.
Don't be glum on Fridays.
On Saturdays, live to the max.
Sundays will be fun days, if you
RELAX! RELAX! RELAX!

If you like MONDAYS
— You'll love TUESDAYS!

I highly recommend DON'T FEED THE MONSTER ON TUESDAYS! to parents and teachers who are genuinely interested in helping their children build self-esteem. Make a child feel special by reading this book to him. It will be fun!
    Robert S. Craig, Ed.D., Psychologist and Clinic Director
       Plainfield Counseling Clinic

Anyone who works with children is aware of the importance of self-esteem. Much has been written about children's self-esteem, but nothing equal to MONSTER has been crafted for young children. The text is easy to read and the illustrations are entertaining. I prescribe MONSTER for every child, because it offers children usable building blocks for a healthy, life-long foundation. Children, child therapists, teachers, and parents alike will treasure this delightfully informative book.
  K.J. Shaffer, M.D., Child Psychiatrist
    Director, Avon Clinic

Adolph Moser knows how to motivate and educate youngsters while simultaneously entertaining them. DON'T FEED THE MONSTER ON TUESDAYS! belongs on the shelves of children's libraries — both public and home.
      Dennis E. Hensley, Ph.D., author
      UNCOMMON SENSE

Every school year should start with having students read DON'T FEED THE MONSTER ON TUESDAYS!. I can't think of a better beginning for children. Try it! You'll like it!
    Bonnie G. Molloy,
    Educator, Parent, Nurturing Grandparent